Original title:
Beyond Heartbreak

Copyright © 2024 Swan Charm
All rights reserved.

Author: Sebastian Sarapuu
ISBN HARDBACK: 978-9916-89-616-7
ISBN PAPERBACK: 978-9916-89-617-4
ISBN EBOOK: 978-9916-89-618-1

Heartstrings Untangled

In shadowed corners where silence drapes,
Whispers of love in delicate shapes.
Threads of the past entwined in our souls,
Yet freedom beckons, as time gently rolls.

Each heartbeat echoes a unique refrain,
Entwined yet distant, joy mixed with pain.
We unravel slowly, like vines in the sun,
Seeking connection, though we come undone.

Reflections in the Dawn

Morning breaks softly, a canvas of gold,
Stories unspoken, yet waiting to be told.
Light dances lightly on dew-kissed grass,
Awakening dreams as the shadows pass.

In the hush of the dawn, all fears fade away,
Each moment a promise, a brand new day.
Colors blend gently, the sky starts to sing,
Life's sweet resilience in each little thing.

Blossoming from Ruins

From ashes we rise, like flowers in spring,
Hope intertwines with the pain that we bring.
A garden of courage where struggle has sown,
Fragrance of healing in seeds we have grown.

The cracks in our armor reveal inner light,
Strength born from darkness emerges in flight.
Through trials we flourish, and yet we still stand,
Together in spirit, united, hand in hand.

The Lightness of Being

Floating like feathers on a gentle breeze,
Moments of bliss come with such effortless ease.
In laughter we find the sweet taste of grace,
Unity blooms in this sacred space.

Surrender to joy, let go of the weight,
Dance with the shadows, embrace every fate.
In the lightness of being, our spirits take flight,
Together we shine, a radiant sight.

In Pursuit of Joy

In fields of gold where laughter sings,
We chase the light on hopeful wings.
Each step we take, a dance of grace,
In every heart, a sacred space.

Through valleys deep and mountains high,
We seek the truth beneath the sky.
In gentle winds that whisper soft,
We learn to rise, we learn to loft.

With every dawn, a chance to rise,
To paint our dreams across the skies.
In simple moments, joy unfolds,
In stories shared, in hearts that hold.

Beneath the stars, we find our way,
In friendship's light, we choose to stay.
Together strong through every trial,
In pursuit of joy, we walk a mile.

So let us dance, abandon fears,
With every laugh, we dry our tears.
In this great quest, we find our peace,
In pursuit of joy, our hearts release.

Restoring the Dignity of Self

In mirror's gaze, we search our soul,
To find the strength that makes us whole.
With tender hands, we mend the scars,
Each story told like shining stars.

Through valleys low, our spirits rise,
With every tear, we touch the skies.
In shadows cast, we reclaim the light,
Restoring hope, igniting the fight.

With every heartbeat, claims our worth,
We learn to celebrate our birth.
In every flaw, a beauty shines,
Restoring grace in tangled lines.

So let us stand, with heads held high,
In unity, we'll reach the sky.
With voices strong, we sing our song,
Restoring dignity where we belong.

Together bound, we rise anew,
Embracing all that we can do.
In love's embrace, we find our place,
Restoring self with tender grace.

Moving Forward

With every dawn, a chance to grow,
We shed our doubts, let courage flow.
Paths unknown await in light,
Embracing change, we take our flight.

The winds may howl, but we stand tall,
With dreams to catch, we heed the call.
Each step we take whispers of hope,
A journey shared, together we cope.

One Step at a Time

In a world that rushes, we take it slow,
One step at a time, watch our spirits grow.
Each footfall matters, strong and clear,
Building a path, we persevere.

With hearts aligned and minds in tune,
We dance with shadows, embrace the moon.
Finding our rhythm in every stride,
Together we walk, side by side.

The Resilience in Each Tear

Every tear is a story, a lesson learned,
In moments of sorrow, our hearts have turned.
From pain arises strength so bold,
The beauty in scars is worth more than gold.

Through storms we weather, we stand our ground,
In each heavy sigh, a strength is found.
With resilience built in the depths of our soul,
We rise from the ashes, beautifully whole.

The Colors of a New Horizon

As night surrenders to morning light,
Colors emerge, banishing fright.
Each hue a promise, fresh and bright,
Painting our dreams with pure delight.

Golden rays kiss the earth with care,
Whispers of hope linger in the air.
With open hearts, we greet the day,
Embracing the colors that come our way.

Unraveled Yet Whole

In tangled threads, we find our place,
Where chaos dances with quiet grace.
Unraveled tales of heart and mind,
A tapestry rich, so beautifully combined.

Though pieces may scatter, we learn to heal,
In fractures of life, the truth we reveal.
With every shard, we gather anew,
Unraveled yet whole, forever true.

Fragments of Resilience

In the quiet, shadows creep,
Hope whispers, secrets to keep.
Through the cracks, light breaks free,
Strength blooms where we cannot see.

A heart once shattered, now whole,
Mending pieces, finding its soul.
Each scar tells a tale of fight,
Emerging bravely into the light.

Time, a healer, tender and slow,
Unraveling dreams, letting them grow.
In the rubble, we rise anew,
Fragments of life, the old and the few.

Nature's song, a gentle guide,
Through the storms, we turn the tide.
Each step forward, a dance of trust,
In resilience, we find what is just.

Together strong, we'll paint the sky,
With colors of courage, we will fly.
Embracing life, in every strife,
We bloom brighter, celebrating life.

Echoes of Forgotten Love

Whispers linger in the air,
Memories dance, a silent prayer.
Two souls once, now drift apart,
Yet echoes remain, etched in heart.

Beneath the stars, a soft sigh,
Promises made, with a wistful eye.
Time may fade the once-bright flame,
But in shadows, we still whisper names.

A photograph, the laughter stays,
Captured moments of yesterdays.
Though seasons change, and paths diverge,
The love once shared, forever will surge.

In quiet corners of the mind,
The haunting melodies we find.
Faded dreams, a bittersweet tune,
Love's reflection beneath the moon.

Yet in the silence, there's grace,
A soft touch, a warm embrace.
Though forgotten might be the song,
In our hearts, it forever belongs.

The Dawn After Dusk

Night's curtain begins to lift,
A promise whispers, a hopeful gift.
Stars wane softly, fading away,
As dawn breaks forth, heralding day.

The horizon blushes, kissed by light,
Shadows retreat, yielding to bright.
Nature stirs from slumber deep,
Awakening dreams, no longer asleep.

In stillness, the world takes a breath,
Ushering life, defying death.
Golden rays paint the sky anew,
Pastel hues, a vibrant view.

Each moment glistens, a brand new start,
Renewed passions, igniting the heart.
The struggles of night, now far behind,
In the dawn, we redefined.

Hope blooms within, like flowers in spring,
As the songbirds welcome the day they sing.
In every heartbeat, a rhythm of trust,
In the dawn's embrace, we rise from the dust.

Rebirth in Solitude

In solitude, the soul takes flight,
Finding whispers in the quiet night.
A garden blooms where silence sows,
In still waters, the spirit grows.

Wrapped in thoughts, the heart reflects,
Seeking truth, amidst the effects.
The world outside may seem so loud,
Yet in stillness, I'm fiercely proud.

Fragile dreams begin to emerge,
With every breath, life's gentle surge.
From ashes, I rise, anew and bold,
The warmth of self-love, a story told.

Roots dig deeper in the lone terrain,
Embracing joy, releasing pain.
In the quiet, I find my way,
Learning to love in a brand new day.

Solitude, a sacred space,
Where I discover my own grace.
Through the journey, I learn to be,
In the silence, I find me.

In the Silence of Goodbye

Whispers linger in the air,
A soft touch, a vacant stare.
All the words we left unsaid,
    Echo softly in my head.

Shadows dance across the floor,
Memories knock upon the door.
In the stillness, hearts do ache,
Silent vows we dared to break.

Beneath the stars, the night is long,
Each heartbeat sings a silent song.
In the void where love once lay,
    I find strength in the decay.

Time unravels, moments fade,
Yet in the silence, I'm remade.
From the ashes of the past,
    I rise anew, free at last.

Tides of Transformation

Waves crash softly on the shore,
Changing tides, forever more.
Life comes in with ebb and flow,
In each surge, we learn and grow.

Seasons shift like whispered dreams,
Nature's dance in sync with streams.
Roots that burrow deep in ground,
From the dark, new life is found.

Chasing shadows, chasing light,
In this struggle, we ignite.
Hope like stars, it guides the way,
Through the night into the day.

Embrace the change, let worries cease,
In the movement, find your peace.
Life's great currents will unfold,
Stories of the brave and bold.

Resilient Blossoms

Through the cracks, a flower grows,
Defying odds that nature knows.
With petals bright, it reaches high,
A testament to how we try.

Storms may batter, winds may roar,
Yet through it all, we crave for more.
Standing tall amidst despair,
Strength is found in roots laid bare.

In the garden of the heart,
Beauty blooms, a work of art.
Each leaf whispers tales of fight,
A dance of hope in fading light.

From struggle springs a vibrant hue,
Resilient souls, we start anew.
In every challenge, we take hold,
Emerging strong, both brave and bold.

The Strength of New Beginnings

Dawn breaks through the darkest night,
Casting shadows into light.
Each sunrise brings a chance to learn,
In the fire, our spirits burn.

With every step, the path unfolds,
Stories waiting to be told.
In the silence, strength takes form,
Hearts united, we transform.

The courage found in letting go,
Seeds of hope begin to sow.
In every choice, a spark ignites,
Guiding dreams through starry nights.

Embrace the change, let worries fade,
In new beginnings, joy is made.
With open hearts and open minds,
We find the strength that love defines.

Healing Like the Seasons

In winter's grasp, we learn to wait,
The silent snow, it heals our fate.
Spring whispers dreams of life anew,
Each bud a promise, fresh and true.

Summer's warmth, it brings us light,
A golden glow that feels so right.
Autumn leaves fall, a tender sign,
Of change and growth, so by design.

Through each season, wounds will mend,
Nature's rhythm, a faithful friend.
With every cycle, pain will fade,
And in its place, new hope is laid.

So let the seasons come and go,
Trust in the journey, feel the flow.
For in the heart, healing starts,
As time reveals its gentle arts.

Embrace the change, the dance of time,
In every note, there's love's sweet rhyme.
And as we grow, we learn to see,
The beauty in our journey free.

Threads of Hope Interwoven

In the fabric of our lives,
Hope is woven, rarely dives.
Each thread a story, strong and bright,
Together shining in the night.

Some strands are golden, filled with cheer,
While others whisper, shadows near.
Yet in the tapestry of fate,
We find our strength, we learn to wait.

Each twist and turn, a lesson learned,
Through trials faced, our spirits burned.
But in the darkness, see it glow,
The threads of hope begin to show.

They pull us close when we feel lost,
Reminding us of what is cost.
With every stitch, our hearts entwine,
Together, we are so divine.

So hold these threads, and cherish well,
For in their weave, our spirits dwell.
In unity, we rise, we stand,
Creating beauty, hand in hand.

Beyond the Veil of Sorrow

When shadows fall and hearts feel heavy,
Beyond the veil, the light stays steady.
In moments dark, we seek the dawn,
A promise kept, a hope reborn.

The weight of loss can coil like vine,
Yet in that pain, our souls align.
Each tear we shed, a river wide,
It carves a path where love resides.

We gather strength from memories dear,
In whispered words, they linger near.
Beyond the fog, the sun will rise,
Each heartache softened by the skies.

So take a breath, let sorrow flow,
For healing comes in gentle throes.
Embrace the journey, let it be,
For beyond the veil, we find the free.

A tapestry of love we weave,
In every loss, we learn to believe.
Together we'll walk through the night,
Into the arms of morning light.

The Wind's Gentle Caress

The wind whispers softly through the trees,
A soothing balm, a gentle breeze.
It carries tales of distant lands,
And lifts our hopes with unseen hands.

In quiet moments, it sweeps us high,
As fleeting dreams begin to fly.
A breath of change, it stirs the air,
Reminding us that love is fair.

Through fields and mountains, it sweeps along,
A symphony, nature's sweet song.
It sings of journeys yet to come,
With every rustle, we feel it hum.

Let go and feel its soft embrace,
In every gust, we find our place.
For in the wind, there lies a truth,
A path to healing, and to youth.

So close your eyes and breathe it in,
Trust in the flow, let hope begin.
With each caress, our spirits soar,
For in the wind, we learn to explore.

The Voice of Rebirth

In the hush, a soft whisper,
Awakens dreams long forlorn.
The earth breathes in new colors,
As dawn greets the day reborn.

From ashes, life finds its way,
Bud and bloom in radiant light.
Hope rises with fire's warm glow,
Casting shadows into flight.

Winds carry tales of the past,
Of struggle, of pain, and grace.
Yet futures are woven in trust,
In every heart's sacred space.

Through shadows, resilience grows,
Embracing the lessons learned.
In silence, a spirit awakens,
For every soul that has yearned.

The voice of the universe sings,
A symphony of life ahead.
In its embrace, we find strength,
In each heartbeat, stories spread.

Dancing with Memories

Whispers of laughter echo bright,
In corners where shadows play.
Each moment holds a time and place,
In the dance of yesterday.

Faded pictures, a gentle touch,
Carried on the breeze of time.
We sway with ghosts both near and far,
In rhythms both sweet and sublime.

Moments captured, sparks of joy,
Illuminate paths that we've crossed.
In the heart, they softly glow,
In every dream that we've lost.

Twirling through the corridors,
Of laughter, love, and dreams untold.
We cherish the flights of our youth,
In the warmth of memories bold.

With every step, we embrace the past,
The laughter, the tears, the grace.
In this dance, we find our peace,
In the echoes time can't erase.

Chasing the Horizon

Where the sky kisses the sea,
Dreams shimmer like morning dew.
With every step towards the light,
We chase the promise of blue.

Boundless journeys lie ahead,
Through valleys paved with gold.
With every heartbeat, we search,
For stories waiting to be told.

The sun dips low, shadows stretch,
Yet hope glimmers in the dusk.
With each breath, we rise again,
In wanderlust, we find trust.

Through storms, we navigate clear,
The compass points to our heart.
Holding dreams as our guiding star,
In this life, we are a part.

Forever onward, bold we tread,
With the horizon in our sight.
In every step, we find our way,
To the stars that burn so bright.

Unraveled, Yet Whole

Threads of life, both frayed and worn,
Tales of joy and woven strife.
In the chaos, beauty unfolds,
A tapestry rich with life.

In moments when faith seems lost,
A light shines through the cracks of time.
We gather strength from storms we've faced,
Each experience, a rhyme.

Apart we may feel at times,
But connections bind us tight.
In the unraveling, we discover,
New paths illuminated bright.

With brokenness comes healing,
In unity, we find our call.
Together we rise from the ashes,
In love, we embrace it all.

For every piece that falls away,
We learn to cherish what we hold.
In being unraveled, we are free,
Crafting stories yet untold.

Whispers of Healing Winds

Gentle breezes carry the light,
Softly dancing through the night.
They murmur secrets, calm and clear,
A healing touch, drawing near.

In the quiet, spirits rise,
Underneath the vast, dark skies.
With each whisper, hope unfurls,
Embracing dreams that softly twirl.

Leaves of autumn rustle low,
In their flight, lost tales bestow.
Nature's voice will softly lead,
Where the heart finds space to breathe.

Through the valleys, over hills,
Feel the air, its warmth fulfills.
Each breath a promise, pure and true,
Bringing peace and life anew.

So let the winds of healing flow,
A gentle pulse, a vibrant glow.
In every whisper, find your song,
A lullaby to help you along.

The Art of Unraveling

Threads of thought begin to fray,
Questions linger, doubts at play.
In the mindset, shadows weave,
Seeking patterns we believe.

With each layer pulled away,
Truth emerges, makes its sway.
In the quiet, clarity shines,
Revealing hidden, tangled lines.

Moments held in tightly spun,
Lessons learned, the battles won.
As we wander through this maze,
Life unveils its subtle ways.

Tapestry of joy and pain,
In our hearts, the two remain.
As we journey, learn to see,
Art of life, just let it be.

In the end, we find our grace,
In the mess, a warm embrace.
Unraveling what once felt tight,
Brings new dawns, a guiding light.

When Stars Refuse to Fade

In the darkness, moments freeze,
Silent whispers ride the breeze.
Stars above, they shine so bright,
Holding dreams in the still night.

Flickering through the veil of time,
Guiding hearts with ancient rhyme.
Each glimmer tells a tale of old,
Of love and hope, of journeys bold.

Yet some nights, they dim and wane,
Clouded thoughts bring hints of pain.
But deep within that shadowed space,
A spark ignites, an endless chase.

When challenges seem to close,
Look above where true light grows.
For even when the world feels cold,
Stars will shine, their stories told.

So keep your gaze on skies so vast,
Hold tight to dreams, let fears pass.
When stars refuse to fade away,
In their glow, you'll find your way.

Cartography of Tender Sorrows

Maps are drawn with hearts, not ink,
Every line holds what we think.
Tender sorrows we embrace,
Charting paths through time and space.

Each tear becomes a gentle line,
Trace the hurt, the love, divine.
In these contours, stories blend,
Healing comes where hearts transcend.

Markers placed on open scars,
Guide us through the nights with stars.
With every twist and every turn,
We find new places, new lessons learned.

These cartographies, not just pain,
In their depths, a sweet refrain.
For every sorrow, joy will meet,
In woven tales, both bittersweet.

So let's unfold this map so wide,
Navigate with love as guide.
For in the cartography's grace,
Tender sorrows find their place.

Midnight Blossoms

In the hush of night's embrace,
Petals glow with silver light.
Whispers dance in airy space,
Stars above shine soft and bright.

Moonlit shadows weave and sigh,
Dreams unfold in gentle tune.
Chasing thoughts that wander high,
Beneath the watchful, smiling moon.

Fragrant hints of dreams anew,
In the stillness softly bloom.
Hope respires, with each dew,
Crafting magic in the gloom.

Each petal tells a tale of old,
Secrets carried in the night.
Hearts entwined with stories bold,
In the garden of pale light.

Midnight bids us all to stay,
In the haven of our thoughts.
As the night begins to sway,
Cradling all that life begot.

From Ashes Rise New Wings

In the silence after fire,
Life begins to softly creep.
From the ground, a new desire,
Where once promises lay deep.

Hope ignites in ashen fields,
Faintest colors start to show.
Nature's strength, the heart it yields,
We find ways to laugh and grow.

New wings unfold in morning light,
Carried by the softest breeze.
From the dark, we take to flight,
Finding peace among the trees.

Every lesson wrapped in pain,
Transforms us into something bright.
Like the sun after the rain,
We emerge, renewed in might.

In the ashes, life will sing,
Every heart can learn to soar.
From the trials, we will bring,
Wonders that we can adore.

The Alchemy of Lost Dreams

In the quiet of the night,
Fragments dance like silver dust.
Once held tight, now takes to flight,
In the heart, we place our trust.

Whispers echo past the years,
Lessons wrapped in tender grace.
We convert our hopes and fears,
Finding strength in every place.

Stars align, a cosmic spark,
Turning shadows into light.
What was lost, ignites the dark,
Crafting visions, shining bright.

In the furnace of the mind,
We create from every tear.
Lost dreams intertwine, aligned,
Showing paths that lead us here.

Alchemy of heart and soul,
Transforming pain into the song.
In each crack, we find a whole,
Resilient, we are ever strong.

Seasons of Acceptance

In the cycle, time does flow,
Each season marks a different phase.
Winter's chill, then spring's soft glow,
Life unfolds in myriad ways.

With the changing of the leaves,
We learn to cherish every hue.
In the loss, the heart believes,
That every end brings something new.

Summer's warmth, a golden charm,
Life's vibrance dancing in the air.
Beating fast, it welcomes calm,
Finding peace in all we share.

Autumn whispers to the trees,
Letting go with grace and ease.
In acceptance, we find keys,
Opening doors to inner peace.

Every season holds a thread,
Tapestry of life's embrace.
In the journey, sparks are spread,
Acceptance lights this sacred space.

When the Clouds Part

In the hush of dawn's light,
Hope emerges from the night.
Softly whispers in the air,
Promises that we shall share.

Golden rays break the gloom,
Chasing shadows from the room.
With each step, the path grows clear,
Guiding us to what we hold dear.

Birds take flight, song fills the sky,
Embracing dreams that soar high.
In this moment, hearts ignite,
When the clouds part, love feels right.

Beneath the vast expanse wide,
Faith and courage coincide.
Together, we'll rise and shine,
With every heartbeat, we align.

So let the storms come and go,
In their wake, true colors show.
For when the clouds part, we find,
Unity of heart and mind.

A Tapestry of Survival

Threads of struggle woven tight,
In the fabric, tales ignite.
Each knot, a story unfolds,
Of courage and strength, it holds.

Patterns formed in grief and grace,
Embracing flaws, every trace.
Colors blend in rich display,
Life's design in bright array.

Moments stitched with love and tears,
Resilience conquers all fears.
Through the storm, we find our way,
A tapestry that will not fray.

In each thread, a heartbeat lives,
Crafted from what life gives.
Through the trials, we emerge,
In unity, our spirits surge.

Together we weave, hand in hand,
Creating a brighter land.
In our journey, strength we find,
A tapestry of the collective mind.

Unfolding Dreamscapes

In the quiet of the night,
Whispers of dreams take flight.
Imagination swirls around,
In this space, magic is found.

Each vision a vibrant hue,
Painting worlds both old and new.
Casting shadows on the wall,
Guiding hearts with every call.

Through the veil of sleep we soar,
Exploring realms, forevermore.
Stars align in silent dance,
In each dream, a fleeting chance.

Waves of wonder ebb and flow,
In the depths, our spirits glow.
As horizons wide unfold,
Stories of the brave and bold.

When we wake, let echoes stay,
Carrying hope throughout the day.
For in the heart of every soul,
Lie dreamscapes that make us whole.

The Echo of Self-Discovery

In silence, I hear the call,
The echo dances through the hall.
Whispers of truths long denied,
In this journey, I confide.

Layers of self begin to peel,
Revealing wounds that start to heal.
Mirrors reflecting back the light,
I embrace the shadows of night.

In the depths, I find my voice,
Choosing love, my heart's true choice.
With every step, I redefine,
An identity, brightly shine.

Through the struggle, I arise,
Gifting wings to once-bound skies.
No longer lost, I find my way,
In the echo, I seize the day.

In each heartbeat, I discover,
The strength that lies beneath the cover.
The echo of self, strong and clear,
A melody I hold dear.

Lights in the Distance

In twilight's hush, a soft glow shines,
Flickering hopes on shadowed pines.
Whispers of dreams we dare to chase,
Guiding us toward a warm embrace.

Stars above in the velvet night,
Telling tales of love and light.
Paths we wander, hearts laid bare,
Finding solace in the air.

Through doubts deep and fears profound,
There's a melody, a distant sound.
Calling forth the brave and bold,
A promise of stories yet untold.

With every step, the brighter they gleam,
Lessons learned, woven in a dream.
Together we rise, hand in hand,
Finding courage in this land.

So here we stand, hearts aligned,
Seeking the light, the ties that bind.
We'll chase the glow, no matter the risk,
For hope is the fire in life's brisk whist.

From Grief to Grace

In shadows cast by tears we weep,
A heart once whole, now buried deep.
Yet in the silence, love will stir,
In whispered winds, the souls confer.

Each memory a bittersweet refrain,
A song of loss, a dance of pain.
Through sorrow's grip, the soul finds space,
Transforming heartache into grace.

Time's gentle hand, a healing balm,
Brings tender moments, quiet and calm.
In every echo, a lesson learned,
With every flicker, the heart is burned.

From ashes rise new dreams so bright,
In mourning's depth, we find our light.
For every ending, a chance to grow,
And find the strength we didn't know.

So let the tears fall, let them flow,
For in their wake, new love will grow.
From grief emerges beauty, pure,
A testament that we endure.

The Map of Moving On

With every step, a road unfolds,
Paths adorned with stories told.
In the distance, horizons gleam,
Sketching out a new-found dream.

Maps of moments, lines that trace,
The journey toward a brighter place.
Lost no longer, we find our way,
Holding on to hope each day.

Through valleys low and mountains steep,
Promises made for us to keep.
Every turn speaks soft and clear,
Embracing change, we shed our fear.

Fading footprints guide our path,
Turning from sorrow, escaping wrath.
With courage leading, hearts in tune,
We dance beneath the crescent moon.

So forge ahead, let go with grace,
In the map of life, we find our place.
With open eyes, we greet the dawn,
Together we grow, together we bond.

Stones into Pebbles

Heavy burdens that weigh us down,
Rough edges turn to soft around.
With every trial, a polish grows,
Transforming stones to pebbles, shows.

Underneath the current's pull,
Strength emerges, powerful.
Time refines what once was hard,
Turning struggles to a card.

In rivers deep, the waters flow,
Carving paths for seeds to sow.
Patience teaches us to bend,
In every journey, learn to mend.

As day fades into twilight's grace,
We gather pebbles, leave a trace.
Each a token of battles fought,
Tokens of wisdom, dearly sought.

So here we stand, lightened, free,
Stones once heavy, now let be.
With every step, we feel the change,
From rough to smooth, we rearrange.

Sculpting Tomorrow's Light

In the dawn of a new day,
We shape the dreams we hold dear,
With hopes like brushes in hand,
We paint a future, bright and clear.

Each stroke whispers of change,
As shadows of doubt fade away,
We carve paths through the silence,
Emerging from night into play.

The colors blend in harmony,
Creating visions of what's to come,
With every heartbeat a promise,
That our journey has just begun.

Building bridges of kindness,
Uniting hearts in the night,
With courage as our compass,
We'll sculpt tomorrow's light.

So let your spirit ignite,
And dance with the rising sun,
Together we'll shape the future,
In the warmth of love, we run.

The Journey Toward Solace

Through winding paths I wander,
Seeking peace that feels so near,
With each step a weight lifts gently,
In the silence, I hear clear.

The echoes of the past linger,
Yet they fade like morning mist,
A calm begins to envelop,
In this stillness, I persist.

Mountains rise on the horizon,
But my heart knows how to climb,
With resolve as my beacon,
I'll conquer the fears of time.

The journey is not just forward,
But embracing all that's behind,
Each moment a thread of healing,
In the tapestry of my mind.

I walk toward the horizon,
Where the skies begin to blend,
Finding solace in the journey,
With each dawn, I transcend.

Forgotten Roads and New Beginnings

Upon these paths once traveled,
Where memories softly lay,
I find the strength in stories,
That shape me day by day.

The roads seem lost in whispers,
Yet shadows speak of the past,
In their echoes, wisdom lingers,
And the lessons hold me fast.

With every step towards the future,
A new horizon calls my name,
Forgotten roads lead to freedom,
A heart, unbound by the same.

Each turn a fresh discovery,
In the wildness of the spring,
I gather hope like wildflowers,
To weave into what life brings.

So here I stand, unyielding,
With the dawn breaking in view,
Embracing forgotten roads,
For they brought me to something new.

Beneath the Surface of Still Waters

Mirrors of silence reflect the blue,
Secrets are held, in depths that are true.
Ripples disperse with a gentle grace,
Beneath the surface, dreams find a place.

Darkness may hide what the heart cannot see,
Each bubble of thought floats free like a bee.
In tranquil embrace, the world falls away,
Beneath the surface, where shadows play.

Whispers of currents flow soft and slow,
Silent reflections of things we don't show.
What lies beneath is a treasure so rare,
In still waters deep, life's layers lay bare.

A flicker of light breaks the quiet of night,
Showcasing the wonders that dance out of sight.
The heart of it all, where the real flows free,
Is beneath the surface, just waiting for me.

So dive with a heart daring and bold,
Into the stillness where secrets unfold.
Embrace the unknown with courage and grace,
Beneath the surface, our dreams we must chase.

Threads of Independence

Woven tightly with intuition,
Threads of strength bind me near,
In the tapestry of my being,
Each stitch whispers loud and clear.

The fabric of my journey,
In colors bold and bright,
I thread through life's uncertainties,
With courage as my light.

Independence like a river,
Flows free and unconfined,
In its depths, I find my rhythm,
A melody intertwined.

With hands embracing my spirit,
I sketch the dreams I chase,
Each turn a dance of freedom,
In my heart, a sacred space.

So let the world stand witness,
As I weave my story true,
Threads of independence,
Creating skies of endless blue.

Landscapes of Remembrance

In fields of gold, the sun will rise,
Whispers of laughter, lost in the skies.
Footprints of time in the soft, warm sand,
Memories linger, forever they stand.

Through valleys deep, where shadows play,
The hearts we cherish will never stray.
Breezes carry the past's tender song,
In landscapes of remembrance, we belong.

Days softly fade, but love remains clear,
In every corner, your spirit is near.
Mountains may crumble, and rivers may bend,
Yet the bond of our journey will never end.

Seasons may change, the colors may shift,
Yet in these moments, we find our gift.
The tapestry woven with threads of our past,
Holds tales of a love, forever steadfast.

So let us wander through memories vast,
In the landscapes of remembrance, hold fast.
Each breath, each heartbeat, a treasure to keep,
In the garden of time, deep roots we seep.

Embracing the Echoes

In the quiet of night, whispers resound,
Memories linger without making a sound.
Footsteps of time on a winding road,
Embracing the echoes, our hearts are bestowed.

Each laugh, each tear, paints a lingering hue,
Stories entwined in the old and the new.
In shadows we walk, where the light has kissed,
Embracing the echoes, of moments missed.

The winds gently carry the calls of the past,
A haunting reminder of bonds that will last.
Through valleys of silence, through mountains of night,
Embracing the echoes, we find our true light.

In candescent dreams that flicker and sway,
The whispers of love guide us on our way.
Through every embrace, every journey we take,
Embracing the echoes, our souls gently wake.

So listen closely; let the stillness unroll,
In the fabric of time, we discover our whole.
With every heartbeat, every pulse that we know,
Embracing the echoes, our spirit will grow.

Lanterns in the Fog

Through swirling mists, soft light will guide,
Lanterns aglow, where shadows abide.
A flicker of hope in the gray of the night,
Lanterns in the fog, illuminating sight.

Each step that we take, a journey unknown,
With whispers of dreams in the fog that has grown.
Courage ignites in the hearts that believe,
While lanterns in the fog teach us to weave.

The darkness may linger, the path may be rough,
Yet lanterns shine bright when the going gets tough.
From the depths of despair, we rise and we fall,
With lanterns in the fog, we stand ever tall.

The glow of each beacon a promise held dear,
Illuminating futures that seem far and near.
In unity we walk, hearts brave and strong,
With lanterns in the fog, we find where we belong.

So let us not fear the mists that surround,
For lanterns do shine as we gather around.
Together we'll travel, through tempest and strife,
With lanterns in the fog, we revel in life.

Embracing the Unwritten

In shadows where whispers play,
Dreams flicker in the gray.
Paths untaken, hearts align,
The future waits, it's our design.

With every step, we write our fate,
Unseen journeys, no time to wait.
Each silent word, a brave refrain,
In the unknown, we find our gain.

Embrace the blank, let spirit soar,
Create the tales we can explore.
In every heartbeat, stories dwell,
The unwritten page, a sacred spell.

Through tangled thoughts, we seek the light,
In shadows, dreams ignite the night.
Let courage be the ink we wield,
In blankness vast, our hearts are healed.

Each moment, a line, we dare to write,
With hope as our guide, igniting the fight.
We weave the threads of what could be,
Embracing chaos, setting us free.

From Ashes We Rise

When embers fade, we learn to breathe,
From shattered dreams, we start to weave.
Through charred remains, we find our way,
Rebirth begins, a brand new day.

In broken pieces, strength ignites,
From depths of loss, we reach new heights.
With every scar, a tale is spun,
From ashes cold, the fire's begun.

With open arms, we face the storm,
In winter's bite, we find the warm.
Each challenge met, a step inspired,
From despair's night, our souls are wired.

With hope renewed and spirits bold,
In hands of darkness, we seize the gold.
From cinders gray, we build our home,
With every sigh, to rise and roam.

Together we stand, unshaken, strong,
In harmony's dance, we find our song.
From ashes deep, our voices rise,
In unity, endless skies.

The Colors of Tomorrow

In shades of dawn, the future gleams,
A canvas wide with vibrant dreams.
Each stroke of hope, a story bright,
Awakening hearts to embrace the light.

With every hue, our visions blend,
In unity, we learn to mend.
The palette vast, with colors bold,
Together we create, a tale untold.

Through whispers soft, the colors sing,
Of love's embrace and joy they bring.
In every shade, a wish appears,
As laughter washes away our fears.

We paint the world with hands entwined,
In spectral grace, a path defined.
With every heartbeat, colors flow,
In the tapestry, our spirits grow.

An artist's heart finds peace in light,
In shadows cast, we write our fight.
With passion fierce, we chase the dawn,
In the colors of love, we each belong.

Threads of New Narratives

In woven tales, our voices meet,
As threads entwined, we craft the beat.
Through stories shared, we form the whole,
In every heart, a vibrant soul.

Each journey marked by tales of old,
With visions bold, and words of gold.
From ancient paths, new routes emerge,
With every step, our hopes converge.

In laughter's echo, we find our place,
Through every struggle, we showcase grace.
The tapestry rich, with colors anchored,
In unity's bond, despair is conquered.

With purpose strong and dreams intact,
We pen our stories, a sacred pact.
Together we rise, a chorus proud,
In threads of narrative, we're vowed.

As chapters turn and pages fold,
We write the future, brave and bold.
In every thread, a life, a song,
In shared narratives, we all belong.

The Laughter After Tears

In shadows deep, the heart did weep,
Yet hope would rise from sorrow's keep.
Through valleys low and skies of gray,
A laugh would chase the night away.

Each tear that fell, a lesson learned,
From grief emerged, a fire burned.
With every storm, a rainbow glows,
A testament to how love grows.

The sun will shine on weary days,
As joy unfurls in countless ways.
In every chime of laughter's sound,
The proof that healing can be found.

Embrace the light when shadows flee,
For laughter shares our history.
In every smile, a heart's repair,
A memory of strength laid bare.

So cherish tears, for they will show,
The depth of love and heart's true glow.
In laughter's wake, we will arise,
With every beat, we touch the skies.

Beneath the Surface of Pain

In silence thick, the shadows creep,
Where whispers of our sorrows seep.
A heart beneath the veil does ache,
Yet from that place, a strength we make.

The surface shatters, cracks appear,
A depth of hurt, a silent fear.
But in the dark, resilience grows,
From pain's embrace, a spirit flows.

Beneath the waves where anguish lies,
The spirit ebbs, yet never dies.
For every wound that's deeply sewn,
A seed of hope is gently grown.

Through troubled waters, we will swim,
Emerging bright when lights grow dim.
In every struggle, lessons dwell,
A journey forged from pain, we tell.

So seek the depths where shadows play,
For light will guide along the way.
Beneath the strife, a strength we find,
A testament to heart and mind.

From Ashen Dreams to Vibrant Paths

In ashes scattered, dreams once known,
A spark ignites in seeds not sown.
From dusty trails where shadows lie,
New paths emerge beneath the sky.

Each step we take, a chance reborn,
From twilight's gloom to hopeful morn.
The past may fade, but we hold tight,
To visions bright, our guiding light.

Through trials faced and bridges crossed,
We find our way, though paths are lost.
In every challenge, courage grows,
From whispered fears, a strength bestows.

So rise from ashes, let dreams soar high,
For vibrant paths are ours to try.
In every heartbeat, hope anew,
Life's canvas waits, it calls for you.

With every dawn, a chance to tread,
On vibrant paths where dreams are spread.
Embrace the journey, feel the spark,
From ashen dreams to leave your mark.

The Rebirth of a Soul

In quiet moments, softly wakes,
A soul reborn through love's retakes.
From fragments old, new strength shall rise,
To touch the sun and claim the skies.

With every breath, a pledge is made,
To honor all that life has laid.
Through trials faced, the spirit yearns,
For every flame, the heart returns.

In storms that shake the very core,
We find the strength to love once more.
With open arms and hearts displayed,
The path ahead is brightly laid.

Through shadows past, we seek the light,
For in the dark, the stars shine bright.
The rebirth whispers soft and low,
A journey wild, where dreams will flow.

So celebrate this life we weave,
In every moment, learn to believe.
For in rebirth, our stories blend,
A tapestry that has no end.

The Heart's Journey Home

In shadows deep, the heart does roam,
Through valleys wide, it seeks a home.
With whispers soft, love calls its name,
Through storms and trials, it stays the same.

A beacon bright, in darkest nights,
Guiding souls to higher flights.
Each step it takes, a promise true,
To lead us back to what we knew.

With every beat, it tells a tale,
Of love and loss, of highs and trails.
In every tear, a lesson learned,
In every joy, a fire burned.

So let it guide, through time and space,
With gentle hands, the heart's embrace.
For on this road, we find our way,
To where the spirit longs to stay.

Searching for New Horizons

With eyes wide open, dreams take flight,
We chase the dawn, embrace the light.
Each step we take, a world to find,
The heart, it yearns, unconfined.

Beyond the mountains, valleys low,
New paths await, where rivers flow.
With courage fierce, we wander free,
In search of what is yet to be.

Each turn unfolds a canvas bright,
Of colors bold, and pure delight.
With hope as compass, we explore,
Discovering what life has in store.

Through trials faced, and joys to share,
We find our strength, beyond despair.
Together strong, we'll stake our claim,
For every heart must seek its flame.

A Symphony of Healing

In gentle chords, the music flows,
A healing balm, as stillness grows.
Each note, a whisper, soft and kind,
Restoring peace to heart and mind.

With every beat, a hope anew,
In melodies, our spirits brew.
The harmony we find in pain,
Transforms the loss, to gain, sustain.

Through every sorrow, love will sing,
A powerful song, the heart does bring.
In quiet moments, strength revealed,
A symphony that time has healed.

Resonating through the night,
A beacon bold, a guiding light.
In unity, we rise and soar,
A song of love forevermore.

Through the Keyhole of Time

A tiny door, a glimpse, a spark,
Through whispered tales, we trace the dark.
Each moment passed, a shadow cast,
In memories held, forever vast.

With every turn, the clock unwinds,
A dance of fate, where truth unwinds.
Upon the winds of ages past,
We seek the lessons, built to last.

The laughter echoes, tears do flow,
In every heart, the stories grow.
Through fleeting seconds, love remains,
In every heartbeat, joy and pains.

In twilight's glow, reflections shine,
A tapestry of life aligns.
Embrace the now, as time unfolds,
Through every heart, the past beholds.

Embracing the Uncertainty

In shadows where whispers dwell,
We tread on paths, unsure to tell.
The fog wraps tight, but hearts ignite,
In unknown realms, we find the light.

With every step, new fears arise,
Yet courage blooms beneath the skies.
We learn to flow, to bend, to sway,
Embracing all that comes our way.

Through twists and turns, the journey goes,
Each moment fresh, like budding rose.
With open arms, we greet the change,
For life's sweet dance is never strange.

We navigate this winding road,
With every burden, wisdom sowed.
In chaos, find the beauty bright,
Our spirits soar, we take to flight.

The unknown is a canvas wide,
With dreams and hopes, let's take the ride.
For in uncertainty, we grow,
And learn to trust the ebb and flow.

Sketches of Tomorrow

With pencil soft, we draw the dawn,
In hues of hope, new dreams are born.
Each line a promise, futures bright,
With strokes of love, we chase the light.

A canvas stretched, horizons wide,
Imagination, our faithful guide.
In every shade, a story blooms,
Echoes of laughter fill the rooms.

We paint the world with vibrant dreams,
In gentle strokes, reality beams.
Each sketch a glimpse of what could be,
In art we find our unity.

Moments captured, fleeting grace,
Each picture tells a new embrace.
Together weaving, life's fine thread,
In sketches bright, our spirits fed.

Tomorrow waits, a blank page bright,
With every heartbeat, we take flight.
In colors true, our hearts unfold,
Sketches of tomorrow, brave and bold.

The Dance of Solitude

In quiet rooms, the shadows play,
Where thoughts can wander, drift away.
A gentle rhythm, sways and flows,
In solitude, the silence grows.

With every breath, a deeper dive,
Within our hearts, we come alive.
In stillness, echoes find their place,
In solitude, we learn to grace.

The dance reveals what lies within,
In whispers soft, our souls begin.
With every turn, we learn to see,
The beauty in our mystery.

We find the strength in being alone,
In every ache, we've gently known.
Through twilight tears and morning sun,
The dance of solitude's begun.

Embrace the quiet, let it be,
In moments still, we learn to see.
With every step, the shadows twirl,
In solitude, a hidden world.

Dreams Reimagined

In whispered thoughts, the visions start,
Dreams take flight, a work of art.
With open eyes, we blaze the trails,
Reimagining what never pales.

Each hope a spark, ignites the night,
In shadows deep, we seek the light.
With vibrant colors, fears we chase,
In dreams, we dare to find our place.

The canvas vast, our futures weave,
In every heartbeat, we believe.
Through every challenge, we will rise,
In dreams reimagined, reach the skies.

With courage bold, let visions soar,
In every heart, a yearning core.
The power lies in what we share,
In dreams reimagined, love is there.

Together we forge a brighter way,
With dreams reborn, we seize the day.
In unity, our voices blend,
Reimagined futures never end.

Shadows of Yesterday's Embrace

In the twilight's gentle glow,
Memories softly flow,
Ghostly whispers in the night,
Holding on to fading light.

Fingers trace the dusty past,
Moments fade, they never last,
Yet the heart clings to the thread,
Of the words that once were said.

Echoes dance in empty halls,
Time retreats as silence calls,
Each lingering sigh, a trace,
Of a love we can't replace.

Clouds above, they weave and swirl,
Within that world, our dreams unfurl,
Yet shadows linger, bittersweet,
In a dance where heartbeats meet.

Hope emerges from the dark,
Igniting once more the spark,
Though shadows weave their tight embrace,
We find strength in love's grace.

A Symphony of Silent Strength

In the stillness, courage grows,
Resilience in the quiet flows,
Through the storms of everyday,
It finds a way, come what may.

Whispers of a muted song,
Remind us we can still be strong,
With every heartbeat, deep and true,
A symphony begins anew.

Beneath the silence, power lies,
In the starlit, endless skies,
We rise each time we fall from grace,
Strength resides in every space.

With every breath, we stand our ground,
In the still, our hope is found,
A thread of light, a force unseen,
In every heart, a silent dream.

Courage sings, though soft and low,
Through fragile hearts, it learns to grow,
In this tapestry of night,
Silent strength ignites the light.

The Quietude of Moving On

With gentle steps, we change our path,
Turning from the aftermath,
In the quiet, truth reveals,
The strength that time itself conceals.

Weight of memories starts to lift,
In the silence, a precious gift,
Lessons learned in dusk and dawn,
Through the stillness, we are drawn.

Each soft sigh, a step away,
Finding peace in a new day,
With every breath, we learn to let,
Our hearts embrace what's coming yet.

Threads of hope weave through the pain,
In the calm, we rise again,
The echoes fade; we trust the day,
In the quietude, we'll find our way.

Leave the shadows; let them be,
In the stillness, we are free,
With each heartbeat, write our song,
In the quietude of moving on.

Reflections in the Shattered Mirror

Fragments of a life once known,
Through shards of glass, we are shown,
Each piece tells a tale of pain,
Yet beauty rises once again.

Glimmers caught in fractured light,
Reveal the truth beyond the night,
In brokenness, there lies a spark,
That guides us through the deepest dark.

Faces blurred, yet still we see,
The shadows of what used to be,
A mosaic of hopes and fears,
Reflections formed through silent tears.

With courage, we embrace the whole,
Every shard, a different role,
In unity, they shift and sway,
Creating art from yesterday.

Though shattered, we are not undone,
In the pieces, battles won,
Through the cracks, light finds its way,
In the mirror, we choose to stay.

In the Garden of Healing

In the garden, whispers bloom,
Soft petals brush away the gloom.
Each flower sings of light and grace,
Time spent here, a warm embrace.

The sunbeams dance on leaves so green,
A testament to what has been.
Roots entwined, they understand,
Here, true peace does gently stand.

With every dawn, new hopes arise,
Beneath the vast and open skies.
Nature's beauty, a healing balm,
In this sacred space, all is calm.

The whispers of the breeze convey,
Encouragement for each new day.
In this garden, hearts align,
A tapestry of love divine.

So stay awhile, let worries cease,
In the garden, find your peace.
For every petal, every tree,
Holds the promise of what can be.

Navigating the Unknown

In shadows deep, the path is unclear,
Yet courage blooms, dispels the fear.
With each step, uncertainty calls,
But hope in the heart steadfastly stalls.

The stars above, they flicker bright,
Guiding souls through the thick of night.
A map drawn not on paper laid,
But in the choices we have made.

Embrace the twists, the turns ahead,
For every road will surely spread.
Each moment, a chance to grow,
Through uncharted waters we must row.

The compass within, it points the way,
Trust it to lead, come what may.
In the unknown, we find our song,
Building the strength to carry on.

With hearts ablaze and spirits free,
We navigate life's mystery.
For in the dark, our dreams ignite,
Together we find our guiding light.

Crafting a New Future

With hands outstretched, we shape and mold,
Visions of dreams yet to unfold.
Threads of hope, we intertwine,
Sewing the fabric of the divine.

A canvas blank, awaits our spark,
Coloring life from light to dark.
Each stroke, a voice, a story told,
In the tapestry, we dare be bold.

We gather seeds of change and growth,
In unity, we make our oath.
To build a world, to light the way,
For future hearts that will someday stay.

With visions shared and dreams combined,
A brighter path is sure to find.
In every step, with every breath,
We craft a life that conquers death.

So let us rise, with purpose clear,
Creating futures we hold dear.
In every heartbeat, every sigh,
Together, we'll reach for the sky.

The Pulse of Possibility

In the stillness, a heartbeat drums,
A whisper of all that yet becomes.
The pulse of dreams, it hums and swells,
In every soul, a story dwells.

Potential dances, a vibrant glow,
In the heart's rhythm, seeds we sow.
A symphony of hopes and fears,
Resonating across the years.

With open arms, we greet the dawn,
Embracing change where dreams are drawn.
Each heartbeat speaks of what's to be,
In the pulse of possibility.

From silence grows a voice so true,
In every moment, we'll renew.
A current flows, unstoppable force,
Guiding our steps along the course.

So listen closely, take your stand,
In the rhythm, we understand.
The future calls, let's heed the sound,
In every heartbeat, hope is found.

The Heart's Quiet Revolution

In silence blooms a tender fight,
Where whispers weave through the night.
Hope ignites the darkest space,
A gentle pulse, a quiet grace.

With every beat, the power grows,
A soft rebellion that bestows.
In unity, our spirits sway,
Charting paths, a brand new way.

Beneath the surface, change will stir,
A symphony without a blur.
Each heart a drum, a steady call,
Together we shall rise and fall.

From shadows soft, new dreams aspire,
As passion fuels the quiet fire.
In every soul, a spark ignites,
Transforming dusk into new lights.

We gather strength in shared embrace,
A revolution etched in space.
With love, we break the silent chains,
To echo hope where courage reigns.

A Canvas of Second Chances

Brush in hand, I paint with care,
Each stroke a wish, each hue a prayer.
Mistakes once made become the lines,
A tapestry where hope still shines.

With every color, stories blend,
A tale of loss, a chance to mend.
The canvas waits, my heart set free,
To splash on hope, to let it be.

In swirls and shades, I find my way,
Renewed with every new display.
A masterpiece from fractured parts,
As art reflects my moving heart.

Each mark I make tells of the past,
Yet here I am, so free at last.
A journey crafted, bold and wide,
Inviting light to turn the tide.

With every glance, new dreams arise,
A canvas bright beneath the skies.
In this space of endless chance,
I learn to grow, to dream, to dance.

Cultivating Inner Strength

In stillness, roots begin to weave,
A silent vow, a heart that believes.
Through storms that come, a voice holds true,
With gentle might, I rise anew.

Each challenge faced, a lesson learned,
A fire within, forever burned.
From whispers soft to roaring might,
I gather strength through darkest night.

With patience sown like tender seeds,
I nurture dreams, tend to their needs.
In every break, a chance to grow,
Resilient spirit, my inner glow.

I rise like sun from night's embrace,
In shadows deep, I find my place.
A garden blossoming with grace,
Cultivating strength, I run the race.

With every step, a chance to roam,
Unfolding paths that lead me home.
In every heartbeat, wisdom sings,
A medley rich of life's sweet springs.

The Transition of Thought

From whispers soft to echoes loud,
Ideas rise, breaking the shroud.
In this space where minds collide,
I drift and dream, no need to hide.

In currents swift, old patterns fade,
With every shift, new paths are laid.
A dance of minds, both young and wise,
Transforming thoughts beneath the skies.

Questions spark like fireflies bright,
Illuminating the path of light.
In every twist a truth embraced,
The journey's flow, a sacred space.

Ideas clash and shift like sand,
Creating worlds at our command.
Each thought a step toward the free,
A symphony of possibility.

In unity, our spirits rise,
Dancing freely in the skies.
Transition's grace, forever sought,
In every mind, the power of thought.

The Art of Letting Go

In the quiet dusk, let it pass,
Memories like whispers, they frail and glass.
Each thought a feather, drift in the breeze,
Freedom found softly, amidst the trees.

Weightless, the heart begins to unbind,
Releasing the echoes that shadow the mind.
Ties softly fraying, a gentle embrace,
In yielding to change, we find our own grace.

Letting go petals, not longing nor pain,
In every lost moment, renewal remains.
Trust in the journey, the path we must take,
For in every ending, new beginnings awake.

Light sets a glow where darkness once reigned,
The courage to falter, yet never be chained.
In each breath we hold, life opens anew,
The art of letting go teaches us to pursue.

A canvas of hope, unmarked and vast,
Creating tomorrow from echoes of past.
With every release, we gather more light,
In the dance of surrender, our spirits take flight.

A Road Once Traveled

Once we wandered where the wildflowers grew,
Each step a story beneath skies so blue.
Paths woven closely, in laughter we'd roam,
The road once traveled felt just like home.

Time painted memories, soft as a sigh,
With echoes of joy, that never say bye.
Each corner a secret, each turn a new face,
In the heart of the journey, we found our own grace.

Footprints of wonder mark where we've been,
In chapters we've written of places unseen.
Yet the road calls us back to the start,
To gather the pieces that linger in heart.

Dusty and worn, the path beckons near,
Each moment a treasure, the memories dear.
With love as our compass, we courageously go,
Forever remembering the road once traveled, you know.

So here stands the journey, together we tread,
In the tales of our past, our futures are bred.
With hope in our hearts, we cherish each mile,
For the road once traveled makes us smile.

Wings of Renewal

In the dawn of new days, we spread our wings,
With dreams like the clouds, freedom it brings.
Emerging from shadows, we taste the sky,
In the light of rebirth, we learn to fly.

Every heartbeat whispers of chances untold,
In the warmth of the sun, our stories unfold.
With colors of courage, we paint the air,
In the flight of creation, we revel, we dare.

As seasons awaken, we cast off the gray,
With each moment shifting, we find our own way.
Gentle like breezes, fierce like a storm,
In the dance of renewal, we break every norm.

Soaring through valleys where dreams take their shape,
In the embrace of the heavens, we learn to escape.
From the ashes of doubt, like phoenix we rise,
On the wings of renewal, we greet the sunrise.

With horizons inviting, our hearts full of grace,
Forever in flight, we cherish the space.
For in every journey, in every bold quest,
The wings of renewal teach us to rest.

Shadows Fade to Light

In the twilight whisper, shadows take flight,
Dancing to rhythms of day turning night.
Yet darkness can teach us, in silence we find,
The courage to face what is left far behind.

With every soft sigh, the sun starts to rise,
Illuminating paths beyond our own eyes.
The night is a canvas, the stars our guides,
In shadows dissolving, life gently abides.

Echoes of hope linger, sweet as a song,
In the cycle of change, we suddenly belong.
Fragile and fleeting, yet bold in its grace,
The light that emerges gives us a new place.

So when the night lingers and doubts start to swell,
Remember that shadows too have tales to tell.
They fade like the mist, in the warmth of the day,
For when shadows retreat, light gently finds its way.

In the symphony played, shadows blend into hue,
A reminder that light always breaks through.
Embrace every moment, both dark and the bright,
For in this grand dance, shadows fade to light.

Moments of Rediscovery

In the quiet dawn, I find my path,
Shadows fade with each subtle laugh.
Old dreams stir, softly they gleam,
Awakening in the heart's warm beam.

Steps in the grass, a whisper of time,
Every footprint, a rhythm, a rhyme.
Memories dance, alive in the air,
Rekindled hopes spark from despair.

A breeze carries laughter from days long past,
Each moment holds echoes, held tight and fast.
With every heartbeat, the present sings,
In rediscovery, joy gently springs.

I search in the mirror, new lines to trace,
Stories of courage etched on my face.
In the stillness, I learn to abide,
Embrace every change that I cannot hide.

The journey unfolds, I breathe in the light,
With each step forward, my spirit takes flight.
In moments of wonder, I choose to believe,
Every day offers a chance to receive.

Whispers of Resilience

In the depths of night, a soft voice calls,
Strength awakens as the darkness falls.
With every struggle, shadows recede,
Whispers of hope become the heart's creed.

Roots dig deeper in the storm's embrace,
Against the winds, we hold our place.
Each tear nurtures the soil of the soul,
From cracks in the earth, we learn to be whole.

Courage blooms where the fear once lay,
Turning ashes to gold in the brightest day.
Through trials faced, a fire ignites,
In the heart of the storm, we find our heights.

Breathe in the strength that rises within,
In moments of silence, our journey begins.
With every heartbeat, a story unfolds,
Of resilience quiet, yet fiercely bold.

In whispers of night, we learn to stand tall,
Trusting the journey through rise and fall.
With each passing shadow, we gather our light,
In the dance of life, we embrace the fight.

Echoes of Tomorrow

In the hush of dusk, futures take flight,
Visions unfurling in the fading light.
Dreams carved in silence, waiting to bloom,
Echoes of what could be fill the room.

A breath, a pause, as time unspools,
Lessons from yesterday, fate gently schools.
With each passing moment, we weave our thread,
The tapestry rich, in colors we spread.

In the heart's chamber, hope softly glows,
Seeds of tomorrow in the present sows.
With open arms, we greet each dawn,
As shadows of doubt linger and are gone.

In the mirror of dreams, reflections arise,
Promises hidden in the vastest skies.
The stars hum gently, their stories to tell,
Of what lies ahead, where our spirits dwell.

With courage as compass, we journey so far,
Navigating paths towards our true north star.
In echoes of tomorrow, our hearts will soar,
Writing the future, forevermore.

Fragments of a Healing Heart

Amid the cracks, light begins to seep,
Through shattered edges, hopeful and deep.
Pieces scatter, yet they shine bright,
Framing the whispers of love and light.

In tender moments, we learn to mend,
Each scar tells a story, on which we depend.
With patience woven in every thread,
In fragments, the heart learns to tread.

The rhythm of healing, a dance so sweet,
Carving paths forward on tender feet.
Unraveled, we rise, embracing the scars,
Finding our strength in the light of the stars.

With every heartbeat, the past fades away,
Resilience born in the light of day.
In whispered echoes, love's promise imparts,
Beauty unfolds in our healing hearts.

So here we stand, united and whole,
Every fragment a piece of the soul.
In the journey of healing, we openly share,
The love that once faltered now fills the air.

The Symphony of Closure

In twilight's glow, we bid farewell,
Memories dance, a silent spell.
Notes linger soft, like whispered dreams,
Harmony fades, or so it seems.

Each chord a tear, a smile, a sigh,
As echoes fade, we learn to fly.
The final bow, a gentle grace,
In the heart's stage, we find our place.

Completion hums, a soothing tune,
Underneath the silver moon.
Together we weave, parting's embrace,
Notes of love in time and space.

The curtain falls, but not in vain,
For every loss, there's boundless gain.
In every end, a start anew,
In closure's arms, we're born anew.

So let the music play once more,
A symphony, applause, and roar.
For in the close, we find the spark,
A melody that lights the dark.

Sailing into New Waters

The sails are raised, the wind is bold,
A journey new, a tale untold.
With faith as anchor, stars in sight,
We venture forth into the night.

The waves will dance around the hull,
A rhythmic song, both wild and dull.
The sea, a canvas, fresh and wide,
With every crest, we take in stride.

Horizons beckon, bright and clear,
With courage strong, we cast off fear.
Each gust a promise, bright and true,
In waters vast, we'll find our crew.

The compass swings, directing fate,
In every swell, we navigate.
Through storms of doubt, we learn to steer,
To sail with open hearts sincere.

Together bound, beneath the skies,
With hope's own wind, our spirits rise.
Across the depths, we strive and glide,
In unity, we'll turn the tide.

Shifting Sands of Time

In desert's hush, the grains will fall,
Silent witness to nature's call.
With every breath, the landscapes change,
The world unfolds, both strange and range.

As hours slip by, like shadows cast,
We hold the present, fleeting, fast.
In twilight's glow, the past does blend,
Each moment holds where journeys end.

Sands of the hourglass trickle slow,
A gentle rhythm, ebb and flow.
We shape our paths with every choice,
Time whispers softly, a guiding voice.

The dunes rise high, then low once more,
A cycle we embrace, explore.
In shifting sands, we find our ground,
In endless time, our hopes are found.

So let us wander, hearts entwined,
Through every shift, the truth we find.
In this vast space, we learn to breathe,
In shifting sands, we dare believe.

Signposts of Change

A crossroads stands, where paths divide,
In every choice, we learn to guide.
With arrows pointing, futures gleam,
A leap of faith, a daring dream.

In every turn, a chance to grow,
With open hearts, we face the flow.
The signs appear, with wisdom's light,
Illuminating the dark of night.

The road ahead may twist and bend,
But with each step, we can transcend.
For change is but a season's dance,
A fleeting chance for hearts to chance.

We'll leave behind our fears and doubt,
For in our souls, there's strength throughout.
With every sign, we forge our way,
In changing times, we find our sway.

So take a breath, embrace the tide,
In signposts trusted, we'll abide.
Life's journey calls, with hope in range,
Together we'll embrace each change.

The Weight of Unseen Chains

Beneath the surface, burdens lie,
Silent echoes, unheard sighs.
Each step forward, heavy sway,
Carrying shadows, day by day.

Invisible ties that bind the soul,
Pulling tight, they take their toll.
Yet within, a fire glows,
Resilience blooms, and courage grows.

In the quiet moments, strength is found,
Breaking free from the heavy ground.
Chains may rust, but not in heart,
For every ending, a brand new start.

Through storms of doubt, the spirit flies,
Unseen winds beneath the skies.
With dreams as wings, we rise anew,
Out of the dark, into the view.

In unity, we all remain,
Understanding each other's pain.
Together we lift, together we stand,
Transforming the weight with hope in hand.

Map of the Heart's Reconstruction

A map unfolds beneath the skin,
Tracing roads where love has been.
Each tear a river, every laugh a bend,
In the journey, we learn to mend.

Rivers of doubt, valleys of fear,
Yet every heartbeat brings us near.
We chart the path with strokes of grace,
Finding solace in every place.

Mountains rise to greet the brave,
Summits called forth by the waves.
Through every loss, a lesson learned,
With each new step, the soul is turned.

Markers of dreams on the way we roam,
Every twist leads us closer to home.
Navigating through the night and day,
The heart's reconstruction finds the way.

In ink of love, the map is drawn,
A testament to hope's sweet dawn.
For every scar, a story flows,
In the journey of the heart, it grows.

Stars that Shine in Empty Skies

In the silence of the night, they gleam,
Whispers of hopes, a distant dream.
Scattered light on a blank canvas,
Guiding souls through the vast abyss.

Each twinkle holds a forgotten wish,
In the void, we find our bliss.
A dance of light in the darkest space,
Offering strength, a warm embrace.

Through clouds of doubt, they pierce the gray,
A beacon bright to light the way.
In quiet moments, their secrets speak,
Filling hearts that feel so weak.

Cosmic gems in an endless sea,
Reminding us how bright we can be.
Though shadows loom and nights may fall,
The stars persist, a constant call.

Their glow ignites our inner fire,
Creating dreams that never tire.
In the solemn depths, they shine so bold,
A tale of hope in the silence told.

A Tapestry of Tomorrow

Threads of time weave rich and bright,
Colors blend in day and night.
Each moment stitched with care and love,
A vision formed from dreams above.

Patterns rise in vibrant hues,
An art of dreams, a world to choose.
With every twist, new stories form,
In the storm, we find our warmth.

Embracing change, we find our grace,
The tangled paths, a sacred space.
Every fiber tells a tale,
Of courage found when hopes seem frail.

Through setbacks, our spirit glows,
In the fabric, strength still grows.
Woven tight, we stand as one,
A tapestry of dreams begun.

So let us stitch the days ahead,
With love and laughter, fear we shed.
For together, hand in hand we soar,
Creating a future to explore.

When Stars Reignite

In the velvet night so deep,
Whispers of love begin to seep.
Flickers of hope in shadows play,
Warming hearts, lighting the way.

Glimmers dance on the darkened space,
Each twinkle holds a soft embrace.
Together we rise like a song,
Echoing where we both belong.

Memories weave through the air,
Binding us with a tender care.
Stars that faded now brightly gleam,
Guiding us back to our dream.

In the cosmos we find our truth,
Rekindled fire, the spark of youth.
Infinite tales in the night,
All around us, a wondrous sight.

When the dawn breaks, we will see,
How the light sets our spirits free.
Under the sun, and the sky so wide,
With stars ignited, we'll take the ride.

Cages Turned to Open Skies

Once locked away in silent fear,
Voices stilled, dreams unclear.
But courage blooms in the heart,
Wings unfurling, ready to start.

With each breath, the chains grow weak,
Hope ignites when the soul will speak.
No longer bound by the past,
We rise together, free at last.

The sky awaits with arms so wide,
Clouds of doubt can no longer hide.
We take flight in the morning light,
Defying shadows, claiming our right.

Feel the wind beneath our wings,
Every heartbeat as freedom sings.
In harmony, we chase the sun,
Together as one, our journey begun.

From cages dark to horizons bright,
We soar on dreams, hearts alight.
With every step, the world unfolds,
A tapestry full of stories bold.

Reclaiming Lost Dreams

In the echoes of forgotten nights,
Whispers linger in faded sights.
Once lost in shadows, we now tread,
Awakening paths that fear had fled.

With gentle hands, we dust away,
The memories that softly sway.
Bright visions call, we hear their plea,
Promising lands where hearts fly free.

Through the fog, we venture on,
Embracing the dusk, welcoming dawn.
Dreams, once muted, now sing loud,
Beneath the sun's warm, glowing shroud.

Each step forward, a seed we sow,
In gardens where our passions grow.
With open hearts, we dare to see,
In every loss, lies destiny.

From ashes rise, our spirits beam,
Finding strength in the thread of dream.
The past may haunt, but it won't confine,
We reclaim our hopes, eternally shine.

Sunlight After Storms

Through tempest winds, we've weathered high,
Each raindrop falls like a gentle sigh.
But after dark, the skies will clear,
Awaiting warmth, a light draws near.

Clouds part slowly, revealing gold,
A promise of warmth, gently told.
In the aftermath, we gather strength,
Emerging from trials, we go the length.

With every ray, new hope ignites,
Watering seeds of future delights.
From storms we've known, we rise anew,
Bathed in light, we embrace the view.

The horizon beckons, vast and wide,
Hand in hand, we walk with pride.
No storm can break what love has found,
In every heartbeat, joy resounds.

As sunlight floods the world outside,
We dance, we sing, no place to hide.
Forever grateful for skies so bright,
In the sun's embrace, we find our light.

Beyond the Wounded Horizon

In shadows cast by falling suns,
The dreams we chased, now undone.
Yet hope remains in whispered sighs,
As stars awake in twilight skies.

Each tear a tale of battles fought,
Of fragile hearts and lessons taught.
Resilience blooms from deepest pain,
A phoenix rising, born again.

Beyond the horizon, wounds will mend,
With every dawn, the darkness bends.
We'll paint the skies in colors bright,
And find our way to newfound light.

Together we'll weave paths anew,
In every heartbeat, dreams come true.
For in our spirits, strength we find,
A tapestry of hope entwined.

So let us walk where shadows pass,
And kindle flames that ever last.
Beyond the wounded, we'll arise,
With courage etched within our eyes.

Forging New Realities

In the forge of thought, ideas collide,
With sparks igniting worlds inside.
From ashes rise, a new refrain,
A symphony of hope from pain.

Brick by brick, we build the dream,
Chasing visions that brightly gleam.
Through trials faced, we learn to grow,
As pathways clear, we start to know.

Hands unite, we craft and mold,
In the crucible, our stories told.
Each twist and turn, a fresh design,
A future bright that's truly mine.

Together we mend the fractured past,
In every heartbeat, shadows cast.
Forging moments that ever last,
Dancing freely, our spirits vast.

With every step, new worlds we find,
In the dance of hope, hearts intertwined.
The canvas waits for colors bold,
A story that's yet to be told.

Harmony After Chaos

Amidst the storm, a tempest roars,
Yet through the pain, a spirit soars.
From chaos springs a gentle tune,
Where hearts unite beneath the moon.

Out of the ashes, whispers rise,
A melody that never dies.
In every crack, the light breaks through,
A symphony of all that's true.

Together we'll find our way back home,
No longer lost, we roam as one.
With every breath, a song we sing,
In harmony, our spirits cling.

The bridge we build is strong and wide,
With love and trust as guide.
To share the beauty deep within,
A journey forged where dreams begin.

And when the calm replaces strife,
We'll dance to the heartbeat of life.
With every note, we mend the scars,
Creating peace beneath the stars.

The Light at the End of the Tunnel

In shadows deep, where hope was lost,
I wandered paths, not counting cost.
Yet in the darkness, sparks appeared,
A flicker bright, a voice I heard.

As whispers of dawn began to rise,
A glowing ember in the skies.
I felt the warmth wrap 'round my soul,
And there, that light began to steal.

Each step I took, a gentle guide,
Through winding roads where dreams abide.
The tunnel long, but I held tight,
To visions sweet of morning light.

Reflections forged in trials faced,
The scars I wear, my strength embraced.
With every heartbeat, truth would swell,
A story of hope I long to tell.

Emerging from the depths I found,
A brighter place, where hearts abound.
The light now glows, forever near,
A beacon bold that conquers fear.

The Language of Letting Go

In whispers of the evening air,
We find the strength to set it free.
The weight of silence fades away,
As shadows dance, we learn to be.

Unraveled dreams in gentle sighs,
A journey starts with every tear.
With open hearts, we learn to rise,
Embracing what we hold so dear.

The past, a tapestry unwound,
We stitch our hearts with threads of light.
In every loss, new hope is found,
The dawn breaks clear, embracing night.

Let go of burdens, let them fly,
Like autumn leaves on breezy trails.
With every breath, we lift our eyes,
And find our way through life's vast sails.

The language speaks, it's soft and bold,
In letting go, our spirits soar.
With every story, gently told,
We find ourselves, and live once more.

Portraits of Unexpected Joy

A child's laugh, a fleeting glance,
In moments bright, our hearts ignite.
We paint the world with every chance,
Lost in the magic of pure delight.

A blooming flower, colors burst,
In simple acts, our spirits rise.
Through laughter shared, we quench our thirst,
For joy is found in sweet surprise.

The warmth of sun on winter's chill,
A stranger's smile that warms the soul.
In little things, we find the thrill,
Of life's embrace, we become whole.

With each new dawn, a canvas bare,
We brush our dreams with hopes anew.
In every step, the world to share,
Creating portraits, bright and true.

Amidst the chaos, still we find,
Those joyful sparks that light our way.
Connecting hearts, the ties that bind,
In unexpected ways, we play.

When the Rain Becomes a Gift

With every drop, the earth will sigh,
As petals dance in puddles wide.
The gray above, a soft goodbye,
Transforms the world in beauty's tide.

In melodies of gentle sound,
We find a rhythm born from pain.
Each storm that churns, rebirth is found,
A precious gift, this sweet refrain.

The air, infused with scents so pure,
Awakens dreams we thought long lost.
Through cloudy days, we find the cure,
In every fall, a gain, not cost.

The puddles mirror skies above,
Reflecting all that we hold dear.
Embracing storms with open love,
We dance in joy, devoid of fear.

When rain arrives, we will not flee,
But run to greet this ocean gift.
In every drop, a symphony,
Our hearts, in tempest, learn to lift.

Melodies of Unfelt Touches

In silence, we connect the threads,
Where hearts unite without a word.
A glance exchanged, the feeling spreads,
In hidden notes, our love is heard.

The warmth of hands that never meet,
Yet linger close in unvoiced dreams.
Each heartbeat echoes, soft and sweet,
In rhythms pulsing, love redeems.

With every breath, a tapestry,
Of whispered hopes and silent pleas.
In moments free from memory,
We flow like songs lost in the breeze.

As shadows dance in evening's glow,
We find the melodies in the dark.
In quiet spaces, love will grow,
Igniting flames, a hidden spark.

Unfelt touches paint our skies,
With hues of longing sprouting deep.
In every glance, a sweet surprise,
Together in the dreams we keep.